# CAMBRIDGE PRIMARY
# Mathematics

## Challenge

**1**

Name: _____

## Contents

**Cherri Moseley and Janet Rees**

CAMBRIDGE
UNIVERSITY PRESS

# CAMBRIDGE
## UNIVERSITY PRESS

University Printing House, Cambridge CB2 8BS, United Kingdom

One Liberty Plaza, 20th Floor, New York, NY 10006, USA

477 Williamstown Road, Port Melbourne, VIC 3207, Australia

4843/24, 2nd Floor, Ansari Road, Daryaganj, Delhi – 110002, India

79 Anson Road, #06–04/06, Singapore 079906

Cambridge University Press is part of the University of Cambridge.

It furthers the University's mission by disseminating knowledge in the pursuit of education, learning and research at the highest international levels of excellence.

www.cambridge.org
Information on this title: education.cambridge.org/9781316509197

First published 2016

20  19  18  17  16  15  14  13  12  11  10  9  8  7

Printed in Spain by GraphyCems

*A catalogue record for this publication is available from the British Library*

ISBN 978-1-316-50919-7 Paperback

This book is part of the Cambridge Primary Maths project. This is an innovative combination of curriculum and resources designed to support teachers and learners to succeed in primary mathematics through best-practice international maths teaching and a problem-solving approach.

To get involved, visit
**www.cie.org.uk/cambridgeprimarymaths.**

# Introduction

This *Challenge activity book* is part of a series of 12 write-in activity books for primary mathematics grades 1–6. It can be used as a standalone book, but the content also complements *Cambridge Primary Maths*. Learners progress at different rates, so this series provides a Challenge and Skills Builder activity book for each Primary Mathematics Curriculum Framework Stage to broaden the depth of and to support further learning.

The *Challenge* books extend learning by providing stretching activities to increase the depth of maths knowledge and skills. Support is given through short reminders of key information, topic vocabulary, and hints to prompt learning. These books have been written to support learners whose first language is not English.

## How to use the books

The activities are for use by learners in school or at home, with adult mediation. Topics have been carefully chosen to focus on those areas where learners can stretch their depth of knowledge. The approach is linked directly to *Cambridge Primary Maths*, but teachers and parents can pick and choose which activities to cover, or go through the books in sequence.

The varied set of activities grow in challenge through each unit, including:

- closed questions with answers, so progress can be checked
- questions with more than one possible answer
- activities requiring resources, for example, dice, spinners or digit cards
- activities and games best done with someone else, in class or at home, which give the opportunity for parents and teachers to be fully involved in the child's learning
- activities to support different learning styles: working individually, in pairs, in groups.

## How to approach the activities

Space is provided for learners to write their answers in the book. Some activities might need further practice or writing, so students could be given a blank notebook at the start of the year to use alongside the book. Each activity follows a standard structure.

- **Remember** gives an overview of key learning points. It introduces core concepts and, later, can be used as a revision guide. These sections should be read with an adult who can check understanding before attempting the activities.
- **Vocabulary** assists with difficult mathematical terms, particularly when English is not the learner's first language. Learners should read through the key vocabulary with an adult and be encouraged to clarify understanding.

- **Hints** prompt and assist in building understanding, and steer the learner in the right direction.
- **You will need** gives teachers and parents a list of resources for each activity.
- **Photocopiable resources** are provided at the end of the book, for easy assembly in class or at home.
- **Links** to the Cambridge International Examinations Primary Mathematics Curriculum Framework objectives and the corresponding *Cambridge Primary Mathematics Teacher's Resource* are given in the footnote on every page.
- **Calculators** should be used to help learners understand numbers and the number system, including place value and properties of numbers. However, the calculator is not promoted as a calculation tool before Stage 5.

**Note:**

When a 'spinner' is included, put a paperclip flat on the page so the end is over the centre of the spinner. Place the pencil point in the centre of the spinner, through the paperclip. Hold the pencil firmly and spin the paperclip to generate a result.

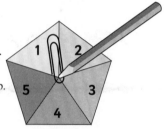

## Tracking progress

Answers to closed questions are given at the back of the book – these allow teachers, parents and learners to check their work.

When completing each activity, teachers and parents are advised to encourage self-assessment by asking the students how straightforward they found the activity. When learners are reflecting on games, they should consider how challenging the mathematics was, not who won. Learners could use a ✓/ ✗ or red/green colouring system to record their self-assessment anywhere on each activity page.

These assessments provide teachers and parents with an understanding of how best to support individual learners' next steps.

# Caterpillar numbers

**Remember**
When you are counting forwards or backwards, the numbers are always in the same order.

Solve each clue.
Cross off the answer on the caterpillar.
The number that is left is the secret number.

It is not 2 + 3.

It is not 0 + 1.

It is not 4 + 5.

It is not 7 + 3.

It is not 2 + 0.

It is not 4 + 2.

It is not 0 + 0.

It is not 2 + 2.

It is not 6 + 2.

It is not 1 + 2.

The secret number is ☐

**Hint**: Use the number track to support counting on.

| 0 | 1 | 2 | 3 | 4 | 5 | 6 | 7 | 8 | 9 | 10 | 11 | 12 |
|---|---|---|---|---|---|---|---|---|---|----|----|----|

Unit 1A Number and problem solving
CPM Framework 1Nn1, 1Nn2, 1Nc1, 1Nc2, 1Nc8, 1Nc11, 1Pt1, 1Pt2; CPM Teacher's Resource 1A: 2.1, 2.3, 4.1

# Aeroplane numbers

Solve each clue.
Cross off the answer on the aeroplane.
The number that is left is the secret number.

**Vocabulary**
0, 1, 2, 3, 4, 5, 6, 7, 8, 9, 10, 11, 12, number, number pair, number bond, count on, count back, add, take away, equals

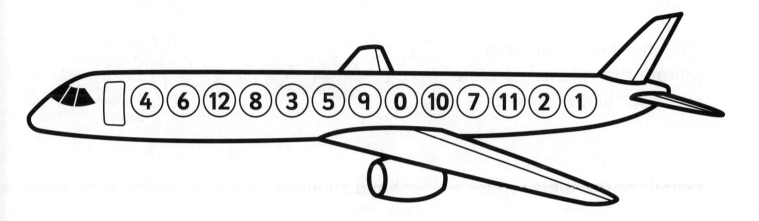

It is not 4 + 3.

It is not 7 – 7.

It is not 3 + 5.

It is not 9 – 8.

It is not 8 + 2.

It is not 9 – 7.

It is not 7 + 4.

It is not 11 – 5.

It is not 3 + 6.

It is not 10 – 5.

It is not 8 + 4.

It is not 11 – 7.

The secret number is ☐

**Hint**: Use the number track to support counting on or back.

| 0 | 1 | 2 | 3 | 4 | 5 | 6 | 7 | 8 | 9 | 10 | 11 | 12 |
|---|---|---|---|---|---|---|---|---|---|----|----|----|

# Hands and feet

**You will need:** a cut-out of your own footprint

## Remember
Do not leave any spaces when you measure.

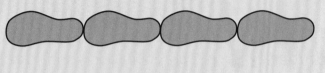

**Vocabulary**
measure, compare, about the same, roughly, length, width

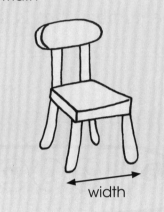

width

Use your hand span and footprint to measure a table top, door and chair seat.

 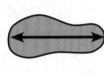

Length of the table top is [ ] hand spans.

Length of the table top is [ ] footprints.

Width of the door is [ ] hand spans.

Width of the door is [ ] footprints.

Width of the chair seat is [ ] hand spans.

Width of the chair seat is [ ] footprints.

Are the measures of each object the same? Explain why.

**Hint**: Keep the hand span the same width when measuring.

**Unit 1C** Measure and problem solving
CPM Framework 1Nn2, 1Nn3, 1MI1; CPM Teacher's Resource 1C 3.1

# Snakes

**Remember**
Do not leave any spaces between the cubes.

**You will need:** a set of cubes all the same size, for example, 2 centimetre interlocking cubes

Use cubes to measure the length of each snake.

**Vocabulary**
measure, compare, long, short, longer, shorter, longest, shortest

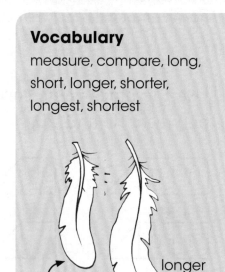

longer

shorter

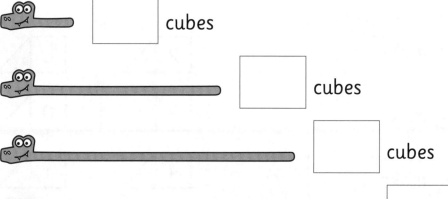

cubes

cubes

cubes

cubes

cubes

cubes

The longest snake is ⬚ cubes long.

The shortest snake is ⬚ cubes long.

Colour snakes that are shorter than your pencil green.

Colour snakes that are longer than your pencil red.

# Tens and ones

**You will need:**

place-value cards for 1, 2, 4, 6, 9 and 10, from resource 1, pages 52–3

### Remember

Two-digit numbers are made from tens and ones. For example, 18 is 1 ten and 8 ones, 10 and 8.

**Vocabulary**

addition, total, digit, tens, ones, place-value cards, arrow cards, lowest, highest

Use the place-value cards to make numbers between 10 and 20.

| 1 0 | and | | make | |
| 1 0 | and | | make | |
| 1 0 | and | | make | |
| 1 0 | and | | make | |
| 1 0 | and | | make | |

| 2 | 6 |
| 9 | 1 0 |
| 4 | 1 |

The lowest number I made is ☐.

The highest number I made is ☐.

Some numbers between 10 and 20 cannot be made with these cards. Write the numbers that cannot be made.

**Hint**: Count from 10 to 20 to find out which numbers are missing.

**Unit 1A** Number and problem solving
CPM Framework 1Nn1, 1Nn2, 1Nn6; CPM Teacher's Resource 4.2

# Numbers to 50

You will need:
resource 1, pages 52–3

**Remember**
The first digit in a two-digit number tells you how many tens, the second digit tells you how many ones.

| 1 | 2 | 3 | 4 | 5 | 6 | 7 | 8 | 9 | 10 |
|---|---|---|---|---|---|---|---|---|----|
| 11 | (12) | 13 | 14 | 15 | 16 | 17 | 18 | (19) | 20 |
| 21 | 22 | (23) | 24 | 25 | (26) | 27 | 28 | 29 | 30 |
| (31) | 32 | 33 | 34 | 35 | 36 | (37) | 38 | 39 | 40 |
| 41 | 42 | 43 | 44 | (45) | 46 | 47 | (48) | 49 | 50 |

Complete the place-value cards for each circled number.

12 is [1 0] and [2] .          31 is [ ] and [ ] .

19 is [ ] and [ ] .          37 is [ ] and [ ] .

23 is [ ] and [ ] .          45 is [ ] and [ ] .

26 is [ ] and [ ] .          48 is [ ] and [ ] .

Circle two more numbers. Complete the place-value cards for those numbers.

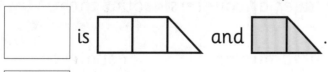

[ ] is [ ] and [ ] .

[ ] is [ ] and [ ] .

**Hint**: Use place-value cards to make each number.

# My hand

**You will need:**
counters, cubes

**Vocabulary**
estimate, count

**Remember**
An estimate does not have to be the right answer.
It is a sensible guess. The more you practise
estimating, the more accurate you will become.

**Hint**: Put the counters or cubes into tens to help to count them.

Draw around your hand.

Estimate how many cubes will cover your hand picture.

Cover your hand picture with a single layer of cubes. Count the cubes.

My estimate ☐ cubes. My counted number ☐ cubes.

Estimate how many counters will cover your hand picture.

Cover your hand picture with a single layer of counters. Count them.

My estimate ☐ counters. My counted number ☐ counters.

Use the words **cubes** and **counters** to complete the sentence:

I needed more _____ than _____ to cover my hand.

**Unit 1A** Number and problem solving
CPM Framework 1Nn2, 1Nn3, 1Nn6, 1Nn8, 1Nn11, 1Pt2, 1Pt9; CPM Teacher's Resource 5.1, 5.2

# Number line numbers

**Remember**
Numbers that are halfway between 2 tens numbers have 5 ones.

**You will need:**
resource 2, page 54

Estimate where each balloon should be joined to the number line.
Draw the string to each balloon from the correct place on the number line.

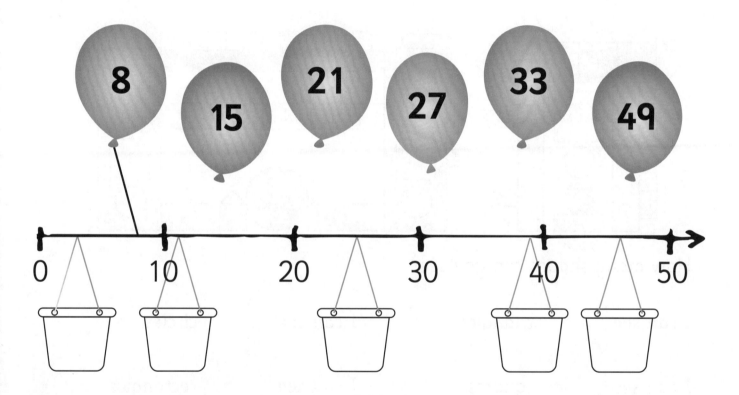

Estimate which number belongs in each basket.
Write the number in the basket.

**Hint**: Use the tens numbers to help.

# 2D shapes

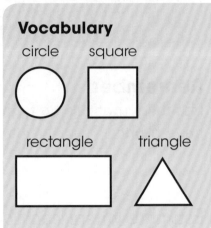

**Remember**
2D shapes are flat.

Look at the climbing frame.

How many shapes can you see?

I can see [ ] triangles.     I can see [ ] circles.

I can see [ ] squares.     I can see [ ] rectangles.

Draw your own climbing frame with
4 circles, 2 triangles, 6 squares and 3 rectangles.

**Unit 1B** Geometry and problem solving
CPM Framework 1Nn2, 1Nn3, 1Gs1; CPM Teacher's Resource 6.1

# 3D shapes

You will need:
everyday shapes

**Remember**
3D shapes are solid.

**Vocabulary**
corner, side, edge, face, 3D

cuboid   cone   sphere   pyramid   triangular prism   cylinder   cube

Look for 3D shapes that are in everyday objects.
Draw or write the name of the shape.

I have
6 flat faces.

All my faces are
squares.

_____

I have
5 flat faces.

1 face is a square
and 4 faces are
triangles.

_____

Choose a 3D shape and
write a set of clues for it.

_____

_____

_____

_____

_____

_____

_____

I have 1 flat face
and
1 curved surface.

My flat face is a
circle.

_____

I have 2 flat faces
and
1 curved surface.

My flat faces are
circles.

_____

# Symmetry

**You will need:** a mirror

## Remember
In a symmetrical shape, each half is a mirror image of the other.

**Vocabulary**
symmetrical

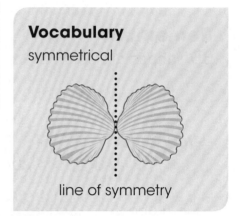

line of symmetry

Add pictures to the right-hand side of the grid to make it symmetrical.

Count the squares from each picture to the line of symmetry. Count the same number of squares, on the other side of the line of symmetry. That is where to draw the matching picture.

line of symmetry

**Hint**: Put the mirror on the line of symmetry to check that the finished grid is symmetrical.

**Unit 1B** Geometry and problem solving
CPM Framework 1Gs3; CPM Teacher's Resource 6.3

# Number spinners

You will need: resource 1, pages 52–53, resource 2, page 54, a pencil and paperclip to use the spinners

**Remember**
Two-digit numbers are made from tens and ones.

**Vocabulary**
number pair, addition, total, digit, place-value cards, arrow cards, 100 square

Spin both spinners to make a two-digit number.
Write the numbers on the place-value cards.

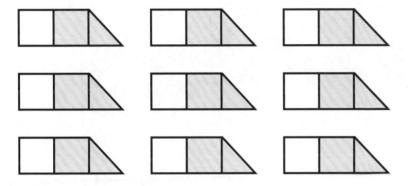

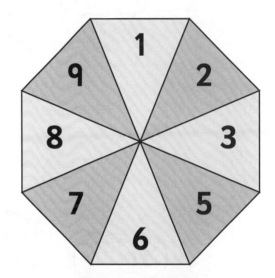

Which two-digit numbers cannot be made?
Write those numbers.
Have you got them all? How do you know?

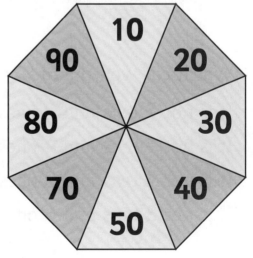

**Hint**: Use the place-value cards to make the numbers.
Use the 100 square to identify numbers that cannot be made.

# Who won the race?

**You will need:**
resource 1, pages 52–3

**Remember**
Two-digit numbers are made from tens and ones.

**Vocabulary**
number pair, addition, total, digit, place-value cards, arrow cards

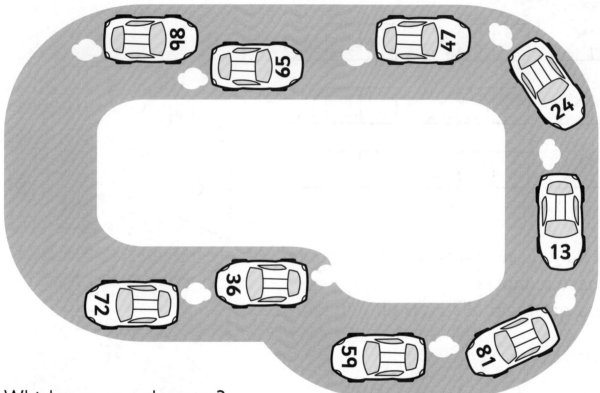

Which car won the race?

It is not 7 tens and 2 ones.

It is not 2 tens and 4 ones.

It is not 9 tens and 8 ones.

It is not 3 tens and 6 ones.

It is not 4 tens and 7 ones.

It is not 6 tens and 5 ones.

It is not 1 ten and 3 ones.

It is not 8 tens and 1 one.

Car number ☐ won the race.

**Hint**: Use place-value cards to make the two-digit numbers.

**Unit 1A** Number and problem solving
CPM Framework 1Nn4, 1Nn6, 1Pt2; CPM Teacher's Resource 7.2

# Oliver's numbers

**You will need:** tens sticks and ones cubes or other base 10 apparatus; resource 1, pages 52–3

Oliver used some tens sticks and ones cubes to make some numbers.

Then he made the matching number with place-value cards.

Do the numbers match?

Change the picture or the number to make them match.

**Vocabulary**
number pair, addition, total, digit, place-value cards, arrow cards

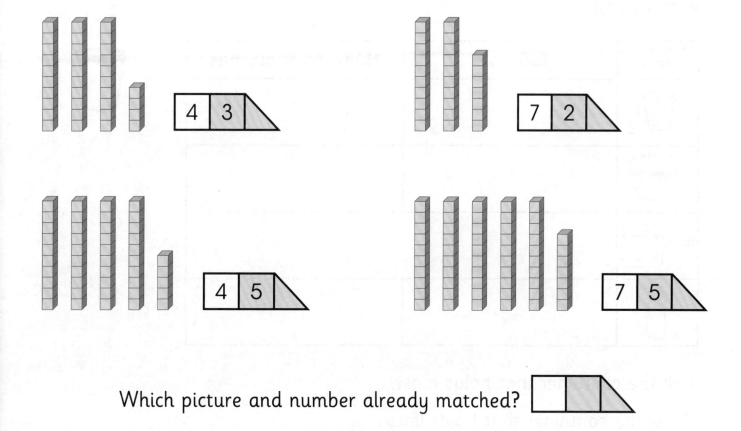

Which picture and number already matched?

**Hint**: Use place-value cards to make the numbers shown by the tens sticks and ones cubes.

# How many cupfuls?

**Remember**
When a container is empty, there is nothing in it.
When a container is full, you cannot get any more in.

**You will need:** a litre jug, small bowl, saucepan and plastic bottle or similar items, plastic cup, counters, water, sand or rice to measure

Estimate how many cupfuls you will need to fill each container.

Now use a plastic cup to see if your estimate was close.

**Vocabulary**
hold, compare, too much, same, estimate, most, least

Record how many cupfuls you needed to fill each container.

| Item | Estimate | Number of cupfuls |
|------|----------|-------------------|
|  |  |  |
|  |  |  |
|  |  |  |
|  |  |  |

Tick the container that holds most.

Circle the container that holds least.

**Hint**: Remember to fill the cup to the top each time. Drop a counter into the container, with every cupful. Count the counters in each full container. The item that took the smallest number of cupfuls has the smallest capacity.

**Unit 1C** Measure and problem solving
CPM Framework 1MI2; CPM Teacher's Resource 8.1, 8.2

# Balancing blocks

**You will need:**
interlocking cubes, balance scales if any are available, or a coathanger with two plastic bags

## Remember
When the scales balance, both sides weigh the same.

**Vocabulary**
weigh, weighs, heavy, light, heavier, lighter, balance, same

Draw lines to join the shapes that you think will balance.

heavier

lighter

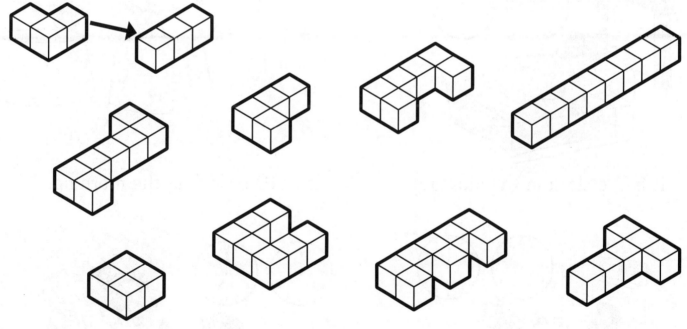

Check on a set of balance scales or a coathanger. If you need to make any changes, use a different coloured pencil.

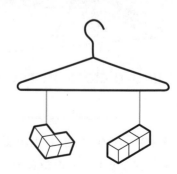

**Hint**: Count the cubes to find out if they will balance.

# The correct time

**You will need:** a clock with movable hands (You could make a clock from a paper plate, a split pin and two cardboard hands.)

## Remember

The **minute hand** is the long hand. It points to the 12 for an o'clock time.
The **hour hand** is the short hand. It points to the hour number.

**Vocabulary**

morning, afternoon, today, before, after, hour, o'clock, clock

Draw a ring around the clock that shows the correct time.

It is 7 o'clock in the morning.

It is 10 o'clock in the morning.

It is 3 o'clock in the afternoon.

It is 5 o'clock in the afternoon.

**Hint**: Move the hands on the clock to show the right time. Check which clock matches.

**Unit 1C** Measure and problem solving
CPM Framework 1Mt2; CPM Teacher's Resource 9.3

# Travel times

**You will need:** a clock with movable hands

## Remember
Count on from the first hour number to the second hour number to find the length of time.

**Vocabulary**
hour, o'clock, clock

How long did each journey take?

**Example:**

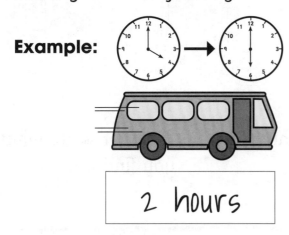

2 hours

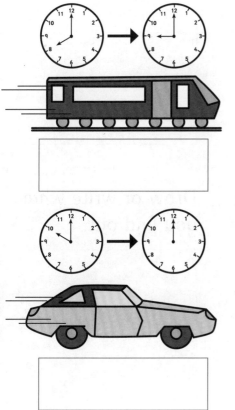

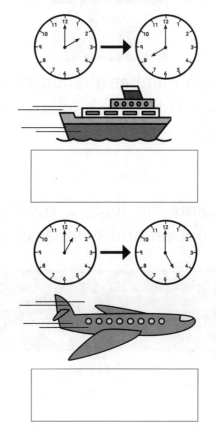

**Hint**: Set the clock to show the first time.
How many hours will it take to get to the second time?

# Chocolate investigation

**Remember**
An even number can always be shared equally between two. An odd number is 1 more or less than an even number.

**You will need:**
cubes or counters

**Vocabulary**
odd, even, pair

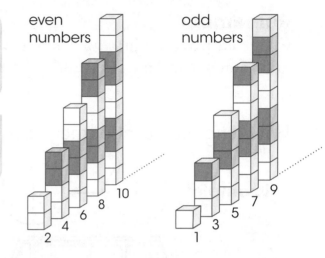

even numbers

odd numbers

Mia and Finn have been given a bar of chocolate.

Mia got an even number of squares and Finn got an odd number. How many squares could they each have got?

Draw or write what you find out.

Another chocolate bar had 12 squares. This time, both children got an odd number of squares.

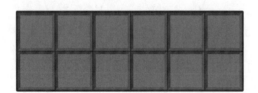

Draw or write what you find out.

**Hint**: Use cubes or counters to represent the squares of chocolate.

**Unit 2A** Number and problem solving
CPM Framework 1Nn5, 1Pt2; CPM Teacher's Resource 11.1, 11.2

# Sharing sweets

**You will need:**
cubes or counters

Arman and Danna were given a bag of sweets.

When they shared them equally, there was one sweet left over.

Sarah, Vasu and David joined them, so they started again and shared the sweets equally.

This time there were two sweets left over.

If there were fewer than 20 sweets in the bag, how many sweets could there have been?

Draw or write what you find out.

There could have been ☐ or ☐ sweets in the bag.

**Hint**: Use cubes or counters to find out what happened.

# Order

## Remember
Ordinal numbers link order with counting numbers.

**You will need:**
a number line
or resource 2,
page 54

**Vocabulary**
ordering, ordinal, ones,
first, 1st, second, 2nd,
third, 3rd ...

Match the numbers with the words.

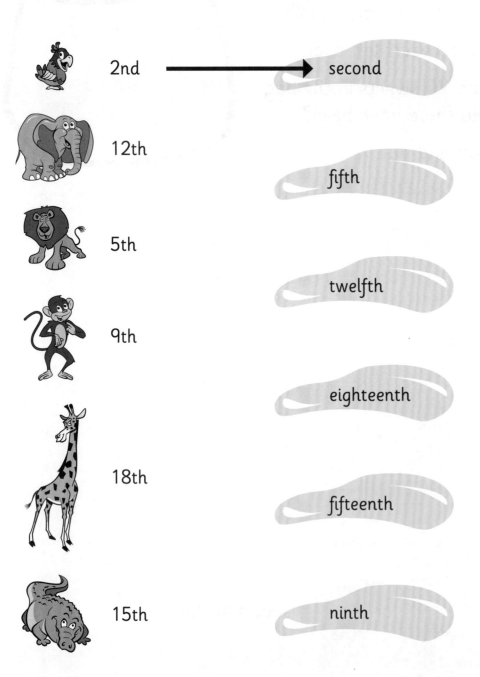

2nd ———————➤ second

12th

    fifth

5th

    twelfth

9th

    eighteenth

18th

    fifteenth

15th

    ninth

**Hint**: Use the number line to check the ordinal numbers.

**Unit 1A** Number and problem solving
CPM Framework 1Nn1, 1Nn2, 1Nn9; CPM Teacher's Resource 12.1

# Ordering numbers

**You will need:**
a number line or resource 2, page 54

**Remember**

When ordering numbers, look at the tens first, then the ones.

**Vocabulary**
tens, ones, less, more, order, smallest, greatest

Put the numbers in each list in order, from smallest to largest.

18, 15, 12, 16

27, 23, 17, 19

28, 34, 26, 31

41, 29, 37, 33

21, 43, 12, 34, 41, 14

Which numbers are between 17 and 20?

Which numbers are between 23 and 29?

Which numbers are between 19 and 22?

Which numbers are between 27 and 33?

Which numbers are between 38 and 42?

**Hint**: Use a number line or 100 square to order numbers and find **numbers between**.

# Missing numbers

**You will need:**
a number line or resource 2, page 54

**Remember**
When you use a number line, jump to the right when adding.

**Vocabulary**
add, addition, altogether

Add the numbers together to find the missing numbers.

*Add 5 and 2 to make 7*

| + | 2 | 7 |
|---|---|---|
| 5 | 7 | 12 |
| 2 | 4 | 9 |

| + | 1 | 3 |
|---|---|---|
| 5 | | |
| 7 | | |

| + | 2 | 0 |
|---|---|---|
| 7 | | |
| 9 | | |

| + | 4 | 7 |
|---|---|---|
| 6 | | |
| 8 | | |

| + | 9 | 0 |
|---|---|---|
| 10 | | |
| 9 | | |

| + | 5 | 2 |
|---|---|---|
| 13 | | |
| 15 | | |

**Hint**: Draw the jumps on the number line to help find the totals.

**Unit 2A** Number and problem solving
CPM Framework 1Nn1, 1Nn2, 1Nc8; CPM Teacher's Resource 13.2, 13.5

# Number paths

**You will need:**
a number line or resource 2, page 54

**Remember**
When you use a number line, jump to the right when adding and jump to the left when subtracting.

**Vocabulary**
subtraction, subtract, take away, less, difference, amount

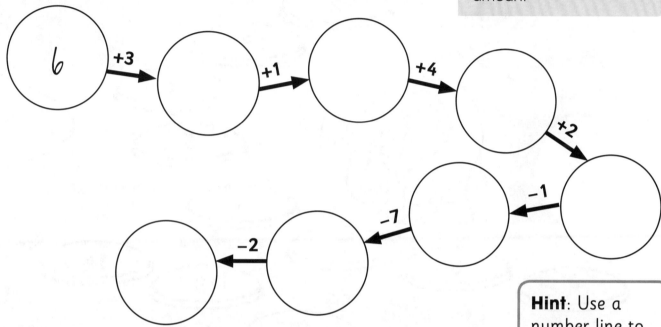

Start with the 6 in the first circle. Move along the path. Follow the direction of the arrows.

Fill in the circles. What happens?

_____

_____

Start with a different number. What happens?

_____

_____

Will this always happen? How do you know?

_____

_____

**Hint**: Use a number line to keep track of the numbers along the path.

**Unit 2A** Number and problem solving
CPM Framework 1Nn1, 1Nn2, 1Nc8, 1Nc9, 1Nc11, 1Pt8; CPM Teacher's Resource 13.2, 13.4, 13.5

27

# Difference track

**Vocabulary**
difference, subtract, subtraction,
take away, less

**You will need:** two different coloured counters or coins, two dice, see resource 3, page 55

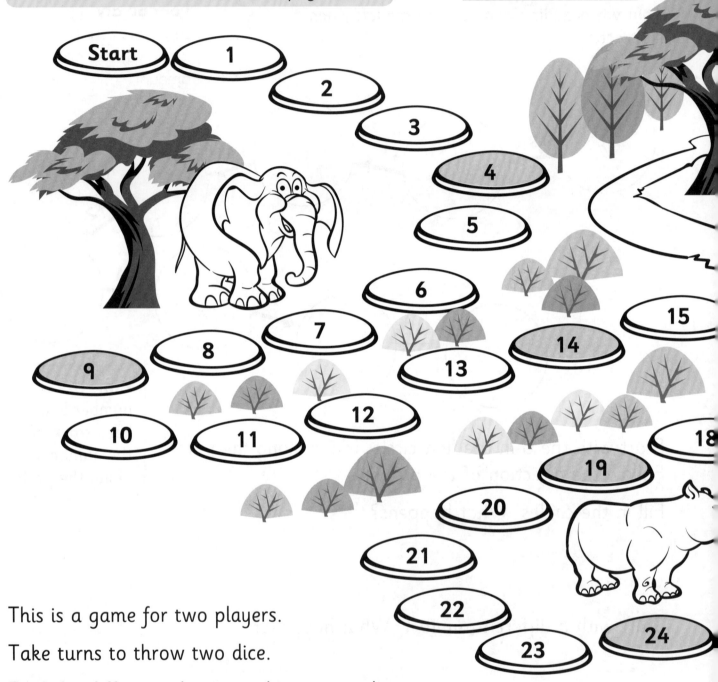

This is a game for two players.

Take turns to throw two dice.

Find the difference between the two numbers.

Move on that number of spaces.

If you land on a shaded stone, miss your next turn.

Who gets home first?

**Unit 2A** Number and problem solving
CPM Framework 1Nn1, 1Nn2, 1Nc8, 1Nc9, 1Nc10, 1Nc11, 1Nc12; CPM Teacher's Resource 13.4, 13.5

**Hint**: Change the rules. For example, 'Land on an odd number, move on 1 space.'

**Unit 2A** Number and problem solving
CPM Framework 1Nn1, 1Nn2, 1Nc8, 1Nc9, 1Nc10, 1Nc11, 1Nc12; CPM Teacher's Resource 13.4, 13.5

29

# Mr Pattern

**You will need:**
resource 4, page 56,
to plan the outfits

**Remember**
Work systematically, changing one object at a time,
to find all possibilities.

**Vocabulary**
combinations, systematic,
possibilities

Mr Pattern likes to wear a different outfit each day. On Monday
Mr Pattern wears a spotty hat, zig-zag T-shirt and spotty trousers.
Draw the patterns to give him a different outfit each day.

| Monday | Tuesday | Wednesday | Thursday |
|--------|---------|-----------|----------|

| Friday | Saturday | Sunday | Monday |
|--------|----------|--------|--------|

**Hint**: Change only one item of clothing at a time.

**Unit 2A** Number and problem solving
CPM Framework 1Pt3; CPM Teacher's Resource 14.2

# Broken 100 square

**You will need:**
resource 2, page 54,
to check against
when finished

## Remember
Two-digit numbers are made from tens and ones.

Each shape is part of the 100 square.

Write the missing numbers in each part of the 100 square.

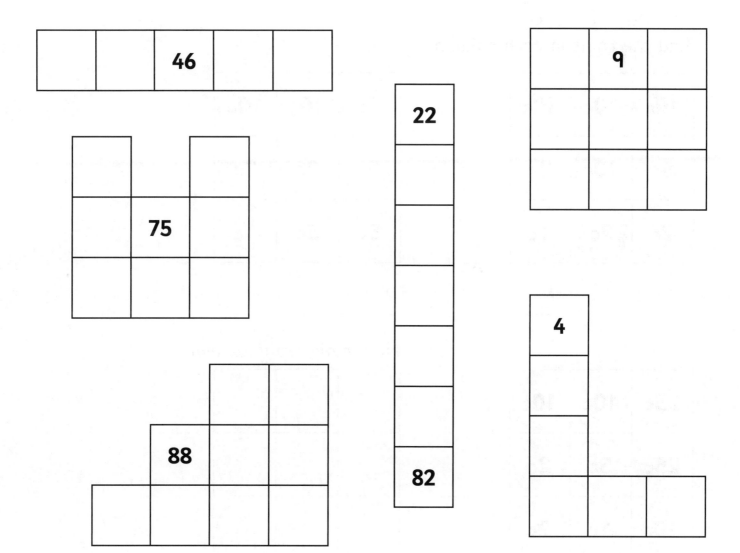

**Hint**: Count in ones along a row and in tens up or down a column.

**Unit 2A** Number and problem solving
CPM Framework 1Nn4, 1Nn6, 1Nn7, 1Pt2; CPM Teacher's Resource 14.1

# Coin grids

**You will need:** coins of all denominations of local currency or resource 5, page 57

## Remember
You can use what you know about numbers to help you add money.

## Vocabulary
money, more, less, how much, total, count, coin, amount

### Example

| | | | |
|---|---|---|---|
| 1c | 1c | 1c | 3c |
| 2c | 5c | 1c | 8c |
| 5c | 10c | 10c | 25c |
| 8c | 16c | 12c | |

Add the coins in each row.
Add the coins in each column.

| | | |
|---|---|---|
| 10c | 10c | 10c |
| 5c | 10c | 2c |
| 2c | 2c | 1c |

| | | |
|---|---|---|
| 5c | 10c | 10c |
| 5c | 2c | 2c |
| 5c | 5c | 1c |

| | | |
|---|---|---|
| 25c | 10c | 10c |
| 25c | 5c | 2c |
| 10c | 1c | 2c |

Now make up your own.

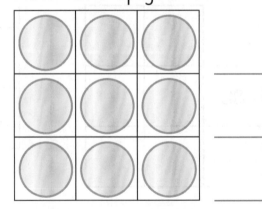

**Hint:** You can use dollars and cents or your local currency.

**Unit 2C** Measure and problem solving
CPM Framework 1Nc3, 1Nc18, 1Mm1; CPM Teacher's Resource 15.1

# How tall?

**You will need:** cubes/squares, ideally 1 centimetre, or use strips from resource 6, page 58

## Remember

When comparing length or height, line up objects edge to edge and from the same starting point.

## Vocabulary

length, long, tall, short, longer than, compare

Use cubes to measure the height of each character.

cubes    cubes    cubes              cubes

On a piece of paper, draw two more characters. Make one taller than the king, the other shorter than the rabbit.

How many cubes tall are your characters? [ ] and [ ]

**Hint:** Start from the bottom of the character and place cubes along the full height.

# Whose drinks?

**Vocabulary**
empty,
nearly empty,
nearly full, full,
least, less, more,
most

**Remember**

A nearly empty jug and a nearly full jug will make a full jug.

empty · nearly empty · nearly full · full

Match the boxes of drinks to the characters.

The kangaroo drinks the most.

The mouse drinks the least.

The king drinks more than the mouse but less than the girl.

The girl drinks less than the kangaroo.

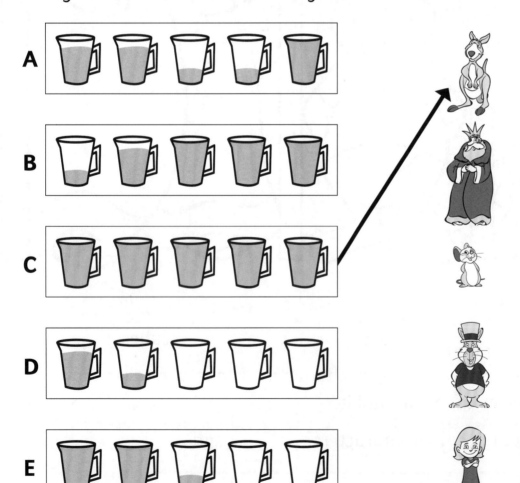

**Hint**: Try putting jugs together.

**Unit 2A** Measure and problem solving
CPM Framework 1MI2, 1Pt2; CPM Teacher's Resource 17.1, 17.2

# Days of the week

**Vocabulary**
day, week, Monday, Tuesday....

## Remember
The days of the week are like numbers, they always come in the same order.

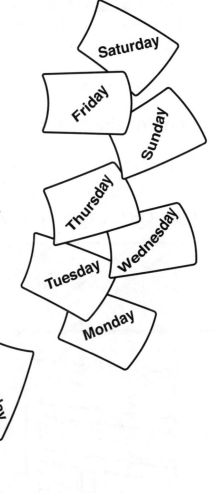

The day after Friday is _____.

The day before Tuesday is_____.

The day after Wednesday is _____.

The day before Sunday is _____.

Complete the table.

| The day before | Today | The day after |
|---|---|---|
|  | Thursday |  |
| Sunday |  |  |
|  |  | Sunday |
|  | Tuesday |  |

**Hint**: Say the days of the week in order to find the **day before** and the **day after**.

# Going home

**You will need:**
a number line

### Remember
Block graphs can be used to sort and group information. A **block graph** gives a picture of how many there are of something.

**Vocabulary**
count, sort, group, set, same, different, block graph

Look at the picture. How is each child travelling home?

Each column in the block graph shows one form of transport. Colour half a square for each child using that form of transport. One cyclist has been done for you.

**Unit 2B** Handling data and problem solving
CPM Framework 1Nn2, 1Nn3, 1Nn5, 1Dh1, IPt2; CPM Teacher's Resource 19.1, 19.2

**Hint**: Cross out the children as you add them to the graph.
Use a number line to count in twos.

Complete the block graph.

1 square = 2 children.

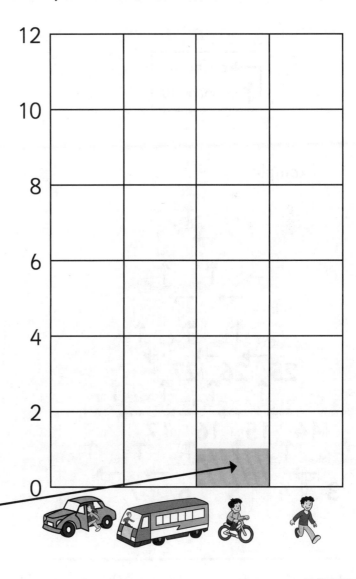

How many children altogether?

**Unit 2B** Handling data and problem solving
CPM Framework 1Nn2, 1Nn3, 1Nn5, 1Dh1, lPt2; CPM Teacher's Resource 19.1, 19.2

37

# Pyramid tens and ones

## Remember

Adding 1 gives you the next counting number. Taking away 1 gives you the counting number before. When you add or subtract 10, the ones digit does not change.

**Vocabulary**

tens, ones, digit, number, place value, partition, more, less, add, subtract

Complete the pyramids as you follow the arrows.

Find the number at the top of the pyramid.

→ count on 1

↑ count on 10

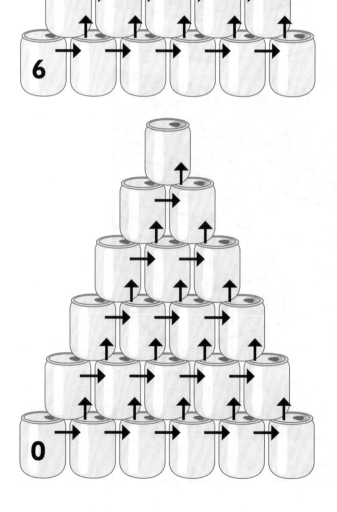

Example:

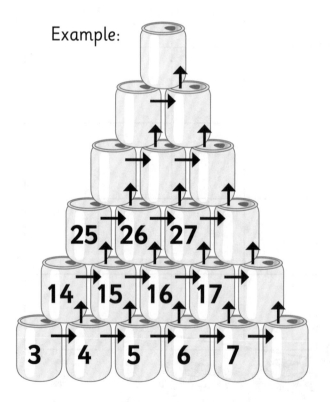

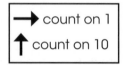

**Hint**: If necessary, use the 100 square to support counting on or back in tens or ones.

**Unit 3A** Number and problem solving
CPM Framework 1Nn6, 1Nn7, 1Nc8, 1Nc9, 1Nc13, 1Pt7; CPM Teacher's Resource 20.1, 20.2

This time the number is already at the top of the pyramid.
What numbers will you write in the bottom row?

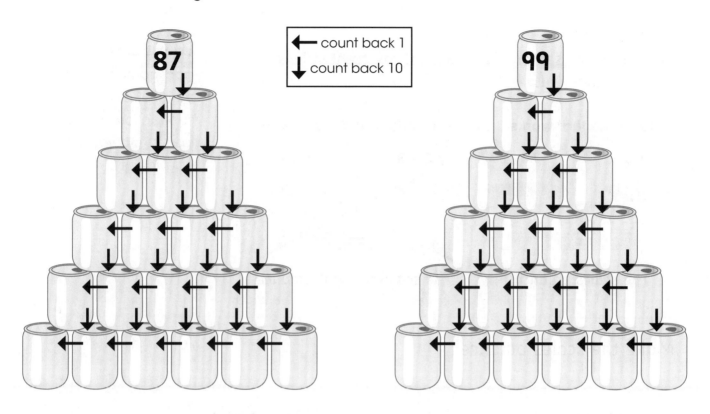

count back 1
count back 10

Now choose your own number to put in the top of each pyramid.
Then fill in the rest of the cans.

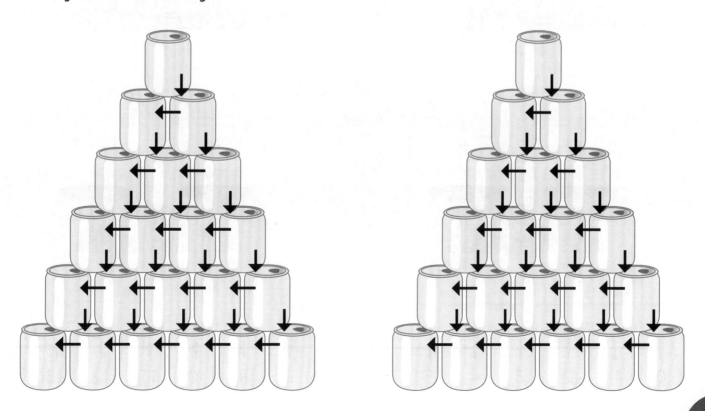

**Unit 3A** Number and problem solving
CPM Framework 1Nn6, 1Nn7, 1Nc8, 1Nc9, 1Nc13, 1Pt7; CPM Teacher's Resource 20.1, 20.2

39

# Balancing scales

## Remember

For a number sentence to balance, the total values on both sides must be equal.

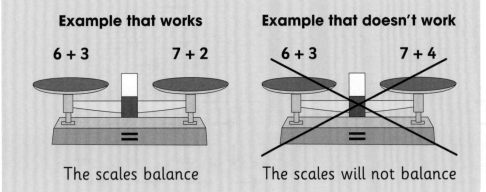

**Example that works**

6 + 3          7 + 2

The scales balance

**Example that doesn't work**

6 + 3          7 + 4

The scales will not balance

**Vocabulary**

add, combine, addition, more, plus, subtract, subtraction, minus, less, take away, equal, equivalent

Make the scales balance.

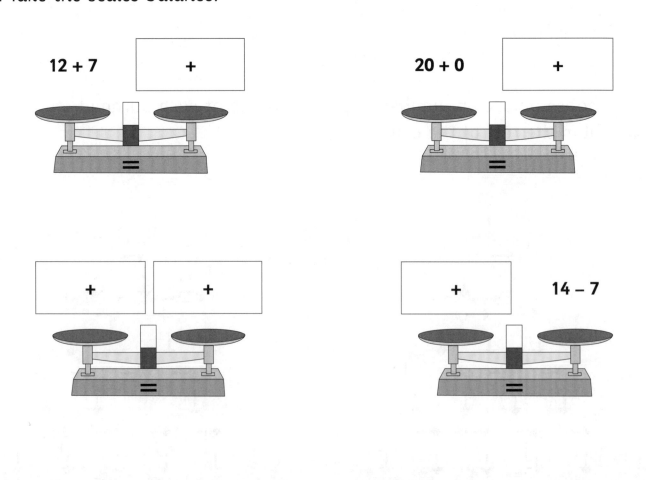

12 + 7     [ + ]

20 + 0     [ + ]

[ + ]  [ + ]

[ + ]     14 – 7

0  1  2  3  4  5  6  7  8  9  10  11  12  13  14

# Make the scales balance.

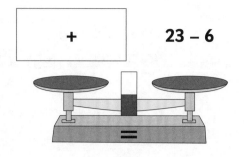

**23 – 6**

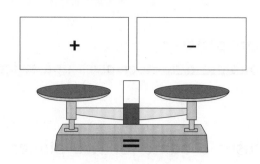

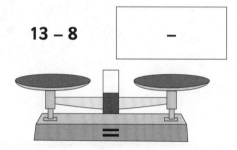

**13 – 8**

**23 – 6**

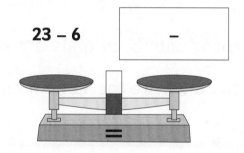

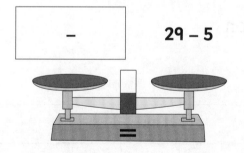

**29 – 5**

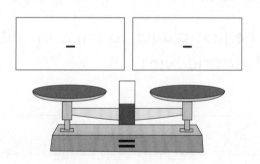

**Hint**: Use the number line to help you find an addition or subtraction calculation to make the scales balance.

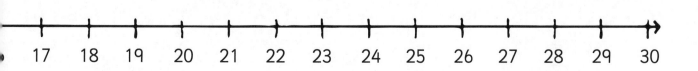

17 18 19 20 21 22 23 24 25 26 27 28 29 30

**Unit 3A** Number and problem solving
CPM Framework 1Nc8, 1Nc9, 1Nc11, 1Nc14, 1Nc18, 1Pt1; CPM Teacher's Resource 21.4

# Troubles with doubles

**Remember**
Doubling a number gives you twice as much.

You will need:
resource 7, page 59

**Vocabulary**
double

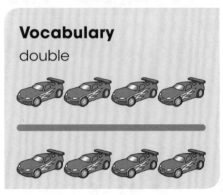

This is a game for two players.

Shuffle the number cards from the resource sheet.

Take turns to turn over the top card, double the number and write the answer in your grid.

Repeat until both grids are full.

You can write the same number more than once.

Shuffle the cards again.

Take turns to turn over a card, double the number and cross the answer off your grid. If the number is not on your grid, miss that turn.

The first player to cross off all the numbers on their grid wins.

| Player 1 | | |
|---|---|---|
| | | |
| | | |
| | | |

| Player 2 | | |
|---|---|---|
| | | |
| | | |
| | | |

**Unit 3A** Number and problem solving
CPM Framework 1Nc19, 1Pt2; CPM Teacher's Resource 22.1, 22.2

# Double or half

**You will need:** counters, a dice or resource 3, page 55

**Remember**

Halving gives you two equal amounts.

**Vocabulary**
double, half, whole, share, fair, equally

This is a game for two players.

| 1 | 2 | 3 | 4 | 5 | 6 | 7 | 8 | 9 | 10 |
|---|---|---|---|---|---|---|---|---|----|
| 11 | 12 | 13 | 14 | 15 | 16 | 17 | 18 | 19 | 20 |
| 21 | 22 | 23 | 24 | 25 | 26 | 27 | 28 | 29 | 30 |
| 31 | 32 | 33 | 34 | 35 | 36 | 37 | 38 | 39 | 40 |
| 41 | 42 | 43 | 44 | 45 | 46 | 47 | 48 | 49 | 50 |
| 51 | 52 | 53 | 54 | 55 | 56 | 57 | 58 | 59 | 60 |
| 61 | 62 | 63 | 64 | 65 | 66 | 67 | 68 | 69 | 70 |
| 71 | 72 | 73 | 74 | 75 | 76 | 77 | 78 | 79 | 80 |
| 81 | 82 | 83 | 84 | 85 | 86 | 87 | 88 | 89 | 90 |
| 91 | 92 | 93 | 94 | 95 | 96 | 97 | 98 | 99 | 100 |

Choose a target number.
This is the target for both players.
Players take turns to roll the dice.
Choose whether to double or halve the number.
Move the counter on by that many spaces.
The player who reaches the agreed target first wins.

**Hint**: Choose a smaller target number for a shorter game. Odd numbers can only be doubled.

# Checking subtraction

## Remember

A subtraction number sentence has two inverse number sentences, for example, $9 - 6 = 3$ has inverse $6 + 3 = 9$ and $3 + 6 = 9$.

**You will need:**
a number line or resource 2, page 54

**Vocabulary**
add, adding, addition, total, subtract, inverse, number sentence

Draw a line to join each subtraction to the addition you would use to check it.

For the last two, complete the checking sentence.

| | |
|---|---|
| | $6 - 9$ |
| $9 - 6$ | $9 + 6$ |
| | $6 + 3$ |
| | $7 + 4$ |
| $11 - 7$ | $7 - 11$ |
| | $7 + 11$ |
| | $9 - 14$ |
| $14 - 9$ | $14 + 9$ |
| | $9 + 5$ |
| | $14 + 7$ |
| $21 - 7$ | $21 + 7$ |
| | $7 - 21$ |
| | $24 + 8$ |
| $24 - 8$ | $16 + 8$ |
| | $8 - 24$ |

| | |
|---|---|
| | $6 + 9$ |
| $15 - 9$ | $15 + 9$ |
| | $9 - 15$ |
| | $6 - 13$ |
| $13 - 6$ | $13 + 6$ |
| | $7 + 6$ |
| | $17 + 9$ |
| $26 - 9$ | $26 + 9$ |
| | $9 - 26$ |
| $29 - 6$ | $6 + \boxed{\phantom{00}}$ |
| $23 - 9$ | $9 + \boxed{\phantom{00}}$ |

**Hint**: Find the solution to the number sentence first, then think how to check that the solution is correct.

**Unit 3A** Number and problem solving
CPM Framework 1Nc8, 1Nc9, 1Nc17, 1Pt6; CPM Teacher's Resource 23.1, 23.2, 23.3

# Balloon addition

**You will need:**
resource 8, page 60

## Remember
You can use number pairs for 10 to make near tens.

**Vocabulary**
near, add, adding, addition, total, number sentence, number bond, number pair

Use the number bonds for 10 and near bonds for 10 to add the numbers in each set of balloons.

Example

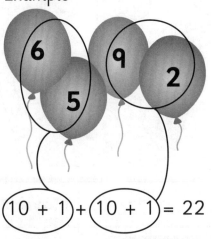

$(10 + 1) + (10 + 1) = 22$

_____

_____

_____

**Hint**: Pair the numbers into bonds for 10 or near bonds for 10.

_____

_____

# Purses

## Remember
Adding money is the same as adding numbers.

## Vocabulary
money, coin, cent (or names of local currency), total

**You will need:**
a number line or resource 2, page 54, coins in local currency or resource 5, page 57, a paperclip and pencil to use the spinner

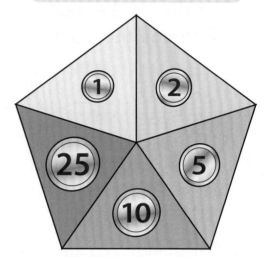

This is a game for two players.
The spinner tells you which coin to take.
Take turns to spin the spinner.
Place the coins on the matching coin purse.
Continue until one player has money in all five purses. The player with more money wins.

| | Player 1 | | Player 2 |
|---|---|---|---|
| 1c | | 1c | |
| 2c | | 2c | |
| 5c | | 5c | |
| 10c | | 10c | |
| 25c | | 25c | |

**Unit 3C** Measure and problem solving
CPM Framework 1Nc3, 1Nc8, 1Nc18, 1Mm1, 1Pt1, 1Pt2; CPM Teacher's Resource 24.1

# Same lengths

## Remember
To compare lengths, make sure that both objects start at the same place.

**You will need:** sticks of 2 cubes in one colour, sticks of 3 cubes in another colour, or resource 6, page 58

### Vocabulary
long, short, just over, just under, about, longer than, shorter than

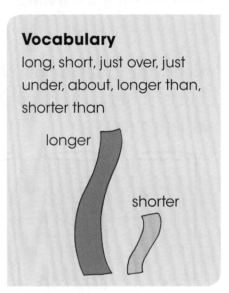

longer

shorter

This is an activity for two people.

Player 1 has sticks of 3 cubes. Player 2 has sticks of 2 cubes.

Player 1 starts with one stick. Player 2 tries to make a stick of the same length.

Player 1 adds another stick to make a longer stick. Player 2 tries to make a stick of the same length.

Continue and complete the table.

| Player 1 (3s) | Player 2 (2s) |
|---|---|
| Number of 3-sticks | Number of 2-sticks |
| 1 | Can't match |
| 2 | |
| 3 | |
| 4 | |
| 5 | |
| 6 | |

What patterns can you see in the numbers in the table?

Alternatively, cut paper strips from resource 6 into twos and threes, discarding any cubes left over.

**Hint**: Focus on comparing the lengths of the sticks after every turn.

# Which glass is left over?

## Remember

To compare capacities, look at the size of each container and how much is in it.

**Vocabulary**

full, half full, empty, half empty, tall, short, compare, container, capacity, holds more, holds less

Read the clues below. Draw a line from each glass to its correct position to find which glass is left over.

| empty | juice | water | juice | water | water | empty | juice |

| 1st | 2nd | 3rd | 4th | 5th | 6th | 7th |
|-----|-----|-----|-----|-----|-----|-----|

## Clues:

The 3rd and 5th glasses are empty.

The 7th glass is tall and full of juice.

There is juice in the 2nd and 6th glasses.

The 1st glass is half full of water.

The 4th glass is tall and full of water.

The 5th and 6th glasses are short.

Draw the glass that is left over.

Draw and label the glass that is left over.

**Hint**: Before starting this activity, talk about the pictures. Use the suggested vocabulary to describe and compare the glasses.

# Earlier and later

**You will need:** a clock with movable hands (You could make a clock from a paper plate, a split pin and two cardboard hands.)

## Remember

When working out a time that is an hour or hours later (or earlier) calculate just as you would with numbers.

**Vocabulary**

clock, hands, hour, o'clock, earlier, later, morning, afternoon

Write the missing times in the grid.

| 2 hours earlier | Now | 3 hours later |
|---|---|---|
| |  | |
| |  | |
| 1 o'clock | | |
| | | 11 o'clock |

Draw a line from each clock to the new time, below.

|  |  |  |  |  |
|---|---|---|---|---|
| 4 hours earlier | 6 hours later | 5 hours earlier | 3 hours earlier | 5 hours later |

**Hint**: Set the hands on the clock to the given time. Use the clock to help you find the new time.

# Sorting toys

## Remember
In order to represent data accurately, work systematically and make sure that you include all the information.

### Vocabulary
count, fewer, sort, group, set, same, different, Carroll diagram

Sort the toys into two sets: those with wheels and those without wheels.

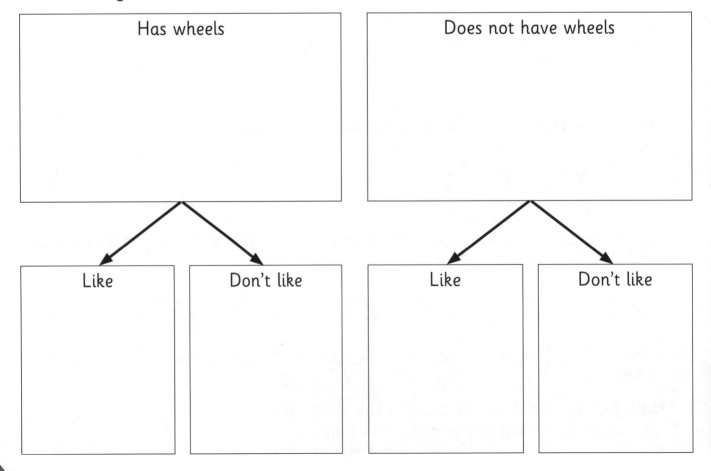

**Unit 3B** Data handling and problem solving
CPM Framework 1Dh1, 1Nn8, 1Pt2; CPM Teacher's Resource 28.1, 28.2

Now you are ready to put the toys into the Carroll diagram.

|  | Like | Don't like |
|---|---|---|
| **Has wheels** | | |
| **Does not have wheels** | | |

Use the words **fewer**, **more** or **less** to complete the sentences.

I like toys with wheels _____ than toys without wheels.

There are_____ toys with wheels than without wheels.

Compare your results with someone else's. How are they are the same?
How are they different?

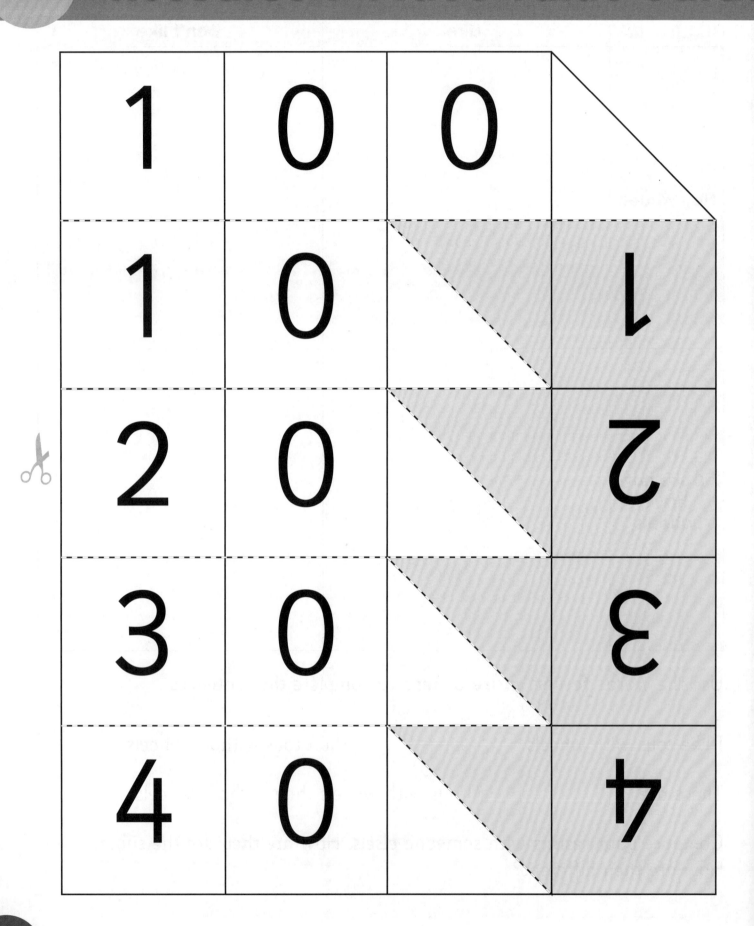

| 5 | 0 | | 5 |
|---|---|---|---|
| 6 | 0 | | 9 |
| 7 | 0 | | 7 |
| 8 | 0 | | 8 |
| 9 | 0 | | 9 |

## 100 square

| 1 | 2 | 3 | 4 | 5 | 6 | 7 | 8 | 9 | 10 |
|---|---|---|---|---|---|---|---|---|---|
| 11 | 12 | 13 | 14 | 15 | 16 | 17 | 18 | 19 | 20 |
| 21 | 22 | 23 | 24 | 25 | 26 | 27 | 28 | 29 | 30 |
| 31 | 32 | 33 | 34 | 35 | 36 | 37 | 38 | 39 | 40 |
| 41 | 42 | 43 | 44 | 45 | 46 | 47 | 48 | 49 | 50 |
| 51 | 52 | 53 | 54 | 55 | 56 | 57 | 58 | 59 | 60 |
| 61 | 62 | 63 | 64 | 65 | 66 | 67 | 68 | 69 | 70 |
| 71 | 72 | 73 | 74 | 75 | 76 | 77 | 78 | 79 | 80 |
| 81 | 82 | 83 | 84 | 85 | 86 | 87 | 88 | 89 | 90 |
| 91 | 92 | 93 | 94 | 95 | 96 | 97 | 98 | 99 | 100 |

# Resource 3 Dice template

Cut out the net, taking care not to cut off the tabs.
Fold along all the lines to make a cube.
Tuck the tabs inside and glue them in place, to hold the cube together.

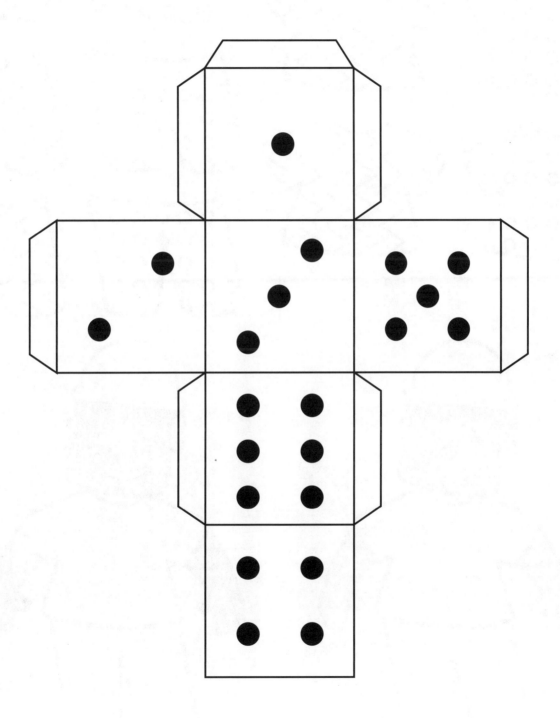

Photocopiable resources

# Resource 5 Coins

# Resource 6
## Centimetre squares

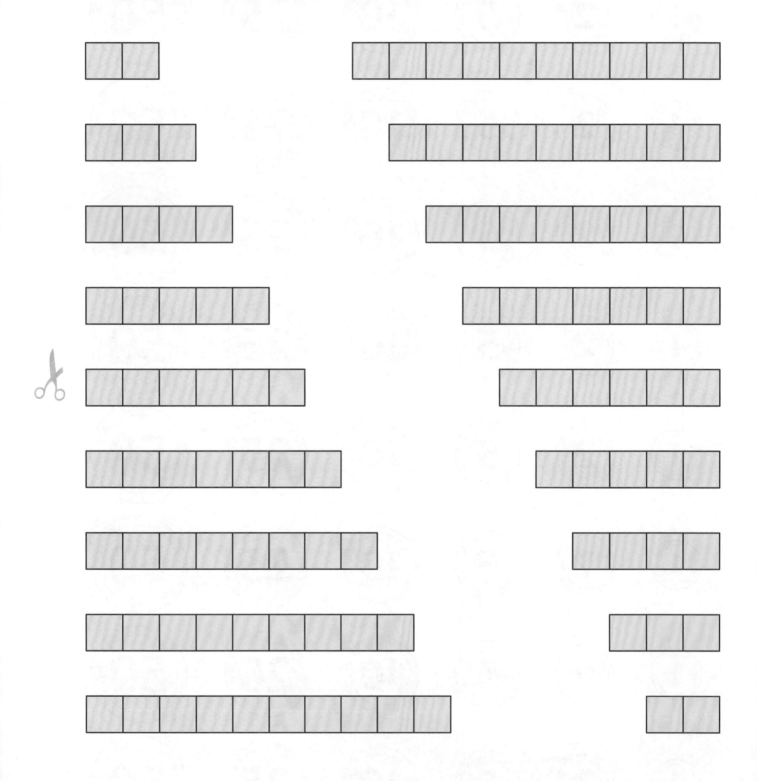

Photocopiable resources

Cut the numbers from the resource and glue them onto thin card, for example, from a cereal box, so that you cannot see the number through the paper.

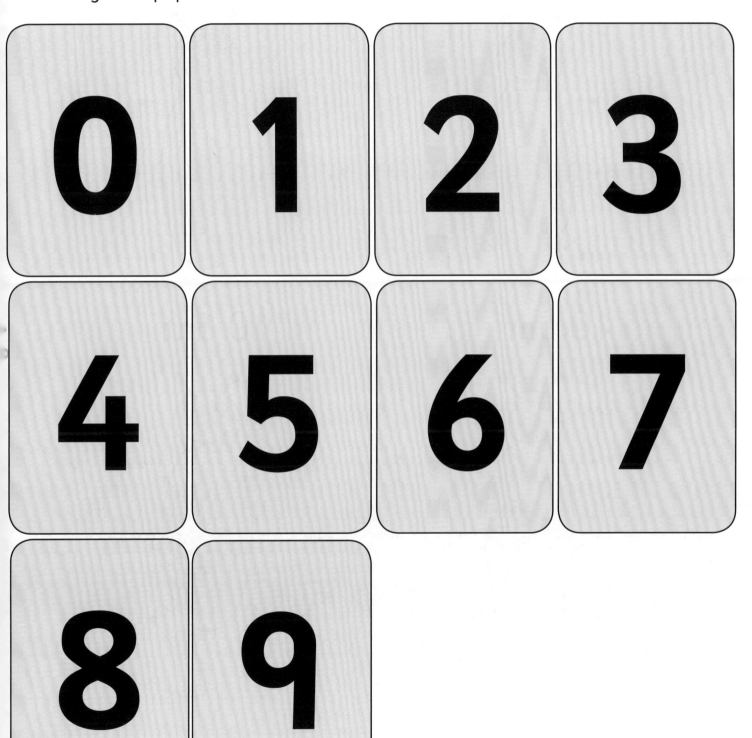

## 10 ant

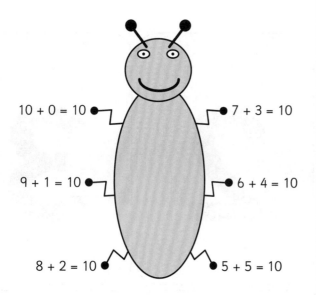

10 + 0 = 10        7 + 3 = 10

9 + 1 = 10        6 + 4 = 10

8 + 2 = 10        5 + 5 = 10

## 10 ant

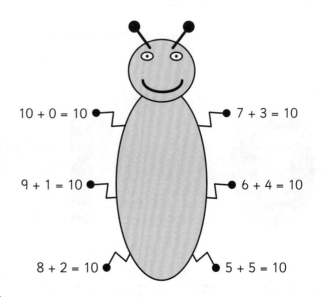

10 + 0 = 10        7 + 3 = 10

9 + 1 = 10        6 + 4 = 10

8 + 2 = 10        5 + 5 = 10

## 10 ant

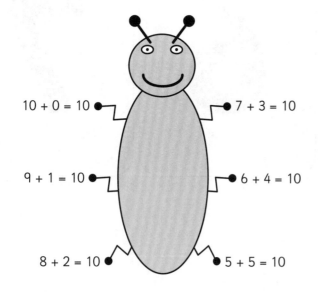

10 + 0 = 10        7 + 3 = 10

9 + 1 = 10        6 + 4 = 10

8 + 2 = 10        5 + 5 = 10

## 10 ant

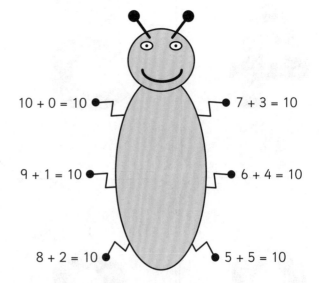

10 + 0 = 10        7 + 3 = 10

9 + 1 = 10        6 + 4 = 10

8 + 2 = 10        5 + 5 = 10

# Answers

### Page 4 Caterpillar numbers
The secret number is 7.

### Page 5 Aeroplane numbers
The secret number is 3.

### Page 6 Hands and feet
Children's own answers. Hand spans may be shorter than footprints, resulting in higher numbers when measuring with hand spans.

### Page 7 Snakes
The shortest snake is 1 cube long (if 2 cm cubes are used).
The longest snake is 7 cubes long (if 2 cm cubes are used).
Other answers depend on the length of the child's pencil.

### Page 8 Tens and ones
10 and 1 makes 11.
10 and 2 makes 12.
10 and 4 makes 14.
10 and 6 makes 16.
10 and 9 makes 19.
The lowest number I made is 11.
The highest number I made is 19.
Missing numbers: 13, 15, 17, 18.

### Page 9 Numbers to 50

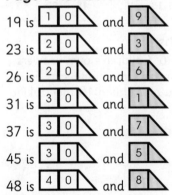

19 is 1 0 and 9
23 is 2 0 and 3
26 is 2 0 and 6
31 is 3 0 and 1
37 is 3 0 and 7
45 is 3 0 and 5
48 is 4 0 and 8

Children's own answers.

### Page 10 My hand
Children's own answers.

### Page 11 Number line numbers

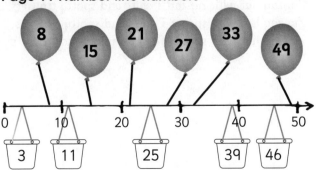

### Page 12 2D shapes
10 triangles
12 circles
24 squares
15 rectangles.

### Page 13 3D Shapes
1. cube, 2. pyramid, 3. cone, 4. cylinder.

### Page 14 Symmetry

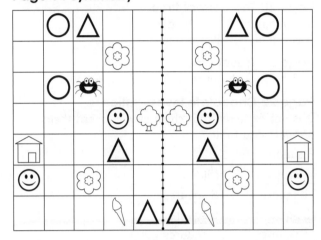

### Page 15 Number spinners
Numbers 61 to 69 and 14, 24, 34, 44, 54, 74, 84 and 94 cannot be made because 60 and 4 are missing.

### Page 16 Who won the race?
Car 59 won the race.

### Page 17 Oliver's numbers
Answers will depend on whether the children decide to change the picture or the number.
1. 34 or 43; 2. 27 or 72; 3. 45; 4. 57 or 75.
Q3 is already matched.

### Page 18 How many cupfuls?
Answers will depend on the containers and plastic cups used.

## Page 19 Balancing blocks

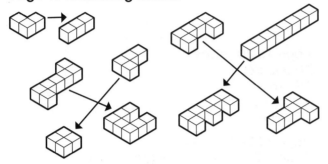

## Page 20 The correct time

It is 7 a.m.　　It is 10 a.m.
It is 3 p.m.　　It is 5 p.m.

## Page 21 Travel times

1. 1 hour; 2. 6 hours; 3. 2 hours; 4. 4 hours.

## Page 22 Chocolate investigation

It is not expected that children will record their answers in a table.

9 squares:

| Finn | Mia |
|---|---|
| 1 square | 8 squares |
| 3 squares | 6 squares |
| 5 squares | 4 squares |
| 7 squares | 2 square |

12 squares:

| Finn | Mia |
|---|---|
| 1 square | 11 squares |
| 3 squares | 9 squares |
| 5 squares | 7 squares |
| 7 squares | 5 squares |
| 9 squares | 3 squares |
| 11 squares | 1 square |

## Page 23 Sharing sweets

7 sweets (1 each) or 17 sweets (3 each).

## Page 24 Order

Parrot 2nd → second
Elephant 12th → twelfth
Lion 5th → fifth
Monkey 9th → ninth
Giraffe 18th → eighteenth
Crocodile 15th → fifteenth

## Page 25 Ordering numbers

12, 15, 16, 18
17, 19, 23, 27
26, 28, 31, 34
29, 33, 37, 41
12, 14, 21, 34, 41, 43
Which numbers are between 17 and 20?
18, 19.
Which numbers are between 23 and 29?
24, 25, 26, 27, 28.
Which numbers are between 19 and 22?
20, 21.
Which numbers are between 27 and 33?
28, 29, 30, 31, 32.
Which numbers are between 38 and 42?
39, 40, 41.

## Page 26 Missing numbers

| + | 1 | 3 |
|---|---|---|
| 5 | 6 | 8 |
| 7 | 8 | 10 |

| + | 2 | 0 |
|---|---|---|
| 7 | 9 | 7 |
| 9 | 11 | 9 |

| + | 4 | 7 |
|---|---|---|
| 6 | 10 | 13 |
| 8 | 12 | 15 |

| + | 9 | 0 |
|---|---|---|
| 10 | 19 | 10 |
| 9 | 18 | 9 |

| + | 5 | 2 |
|---|---|---|
| 13 | 18 | 15 |
| 15 | 20 | 17 |

## Page 27 Number paths

6, 9, 10, 14, 16, 15, 8, 6. Children's own answers. You will always finish on the same number as you started with because you are adding 10 then taking away 10.

## Page 28–29 Difference track

Game – no answers.

## Page 30 Mr Pattern

Mr Pattern dressed in:
Spotty hat with zig-zag T-shirt and zig-zag trousers.
Spotty hat with spotty T-shirt and spotty trousers.
Spotty hat with spotty T-shirt and zig-zag trousers.
Zig-zag hat with zig-zag T-shirt and zig-zag trousers.
Zig-zag hat with zig-zag T-shirt and spotty trousers.
Zig-zag hat with spotty T-shirt and spotty trousers.
Zig-zag hat with spotty T-shirt and zig-zag trousers.

## Page 31 Broken 100 square

| 44 | 45 | 46 | 47 | 48 |
|----|----|----|----|----|

| 64 |    | 66 |
|----|----|----|
| 74 | 75 | 76 |
| 84 | 85 | 86 |

|    | 79 | 80 |
|----|----|----|
|    | 88 | 89 | 90 |
| 97 | 98 | 99 | 100 |

| 22 |
|----|
| 32 |
| 42 |
| 52 |
| 62 |
| 72 |
| 82 |

|    | 8  | 9  | 10 |
|----|----|----|----|
|    | 18 | 19 | 20 |
|    | 28 | 29 | 30 |

| 4  |
|----|
| 14 |
| 24 |
| 34 | 35 | 36 |

## Page 32 Coin grids

| 10c | 10c | 10c | 30c |
|-----|-----|-----|-----|
| 5c  | 10c | 2c  | 17c |
| 2c  | 2c  | 1c  | 5c  |
| 17c | 22c | 13c |     |

| 5c  | 10c | 10c | 25c |
|-----|-----|-----|-----|
| 5c  | 2c  | 2c  | 9c  |
| 5c  | 5c  | 1c  | 11c |
| 15c | 17c | 13c |     |

| 25c | 10c | 10c | 45c |
|-----|-----|-----|-----|
| 25c | 5c  | 2c  | 32c |
| 10c | 1c  | 2c  | 13c |
| 60c | 16c | 14c |     |

Children's own grid.

## Page 33 How tall?
Using 1 cm cubes or squares:
Girl: 6 cubes or squares.
Mouse: 4 cubes or squares.
Rabbit: 10 cubes or squares.
King: 16 cubes or squares.

## Page 34 Whose drinks?
King drinks set A.
Mouse drinks set D.
Girl drinks set B.
Rabbit drinks set E.
Kangaroo drinks set C.

## Page 35 Days of the week
The day after Friday is Saturday.
The day before Tuesday is Monday.
The day after Wednesday is Thursday.
The day before Sunday is Saturday.

Complete the table.

| The day before | Today | The day after |
|----------------|-------|---------------|
| Wednesday | Thursday | Friday |
| Sunday | Monday | Tuesday |
| Friday | Saturday | Sunday |
| Monday | Tuesday | Wednesday |

## Pages 36–37 Going home

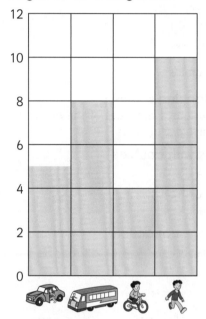

How many children altogether? 27.

## Pages 38–39 Pyramid tens and ones
Completed pyramids:

```
              58
           47  48
         36  37  38
       25  26  27  28
     14  15  16  17  18
   3   4   5   6   7   8

              61
           50  51
         39  40  41
       28  29  30  31
     17  18  19  20  21
   6   7   8   9  10  11

              55
           44  45
         33  34  35
       22  23  24  25
     11  12  13  14  15
   0   1   2   3   4   5
```

**87**
76  77
65  66  67
54  55  56  57
43  44  45  46  47
32  33  34  35  36  37

**99**
89  90
77  78  79
66  67  68  69
55  56  57  58  59
44  45  46  47  48  49

Children's own pyramids.

## Pages 40–41 Balancing scales
Children's own solutions. Both sides of the balance scales must be equivalent in value.

## Page 42 Troubles with doubles
Game – no answers.

## Page 43 Double or half
Game – no answers.

## Page 44 Checking subtraction

$9 - 6 \longrightarrow 6 + 3$.

$11 - 7 \longrightarrow 7 + 4$

$14 - 9 \longrightarrow 9 + 5$

$21 - 7 \longrightarrow 14 + 7$

$24 - 8 \longrightarrow 16 + 8$

$15 - 9 \longrightarrow 6 + 9$

$13 - 6 \longrightarrow 7 + 6$

$26 - 9 \longrightarrow 17 + 9$

$29 - 6 \longrightarrow 6 + \textbf{23}$

$23 - 9 \longrightarrow 9 + \textbf{14}$

## Page 45 Balloon addition
Set 2: $6 + 5 + 9 + 2$
$10 + 1 + 10 + 1 = 22$
Set 3: $1 + 6 + 3 + 9$
$10 + 9 = 19$ or $9 + 10 = 19$
Set 4: $7 + 4 + 0 + 9$
$10 + 1 + 9 = 20$
Set 5: $8 + 5 + 4 + 1$
$8 + 10 = 18$ or $9 + 9 = 18$
Set 6: $8 + 3 + 5 + 6$
$10 + 1 + 10 + 1 = 22$

## Page 46 Purses
Game – no answers.

## Page 47 Same lengths
3 twos is the same length as 2 threes.
6 twos is the same length as 4 threes.
9 twos is the same length as 6 threes.
12 twos is the same length as 8 threes, and so on.
Each new matching length is reached when another 3 twos and 2 threes have been added.

## Page 48 Which glass is left over?

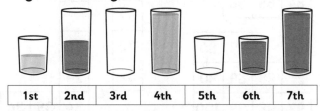

| 1st | 2nd | 3rd | 4th | 5th | 6th | 7th |

6th rule – 5th and 6th glasses are short, therefore there are no swappable glasses.

Leftover glass is

## Page 49 Earlier and later

| 2 hours earlier | Now | 3 hours later |
| --- | --- | --- |
| 2 o'clock | | 7 o'clock |
| 7 o'clock | | 12 o'clock |
| 1 o'clock | 3 o'clock | 6 o'clock |
| 6 o'clock | 8 o'clock | 11 o'clock |

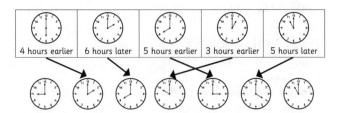

## Pages 50–51 Sorting toys
Children's own answers.
There are fewer toys with wheels than without wheels.